WHEN MOUNTAINS WON'T MOVE

Books by Jacob Hawk

Image of the Invisible God

The Hawk's Nest

Jacob Hawk

When
MOUNTAINS
Won't
MOVE

HOW TO SURVIVE A STRUGGLING FAITH

ISBN-10: 1941972284
ISBN-13: 978-1941972281

Library of Congress Control Number: 2014954978

Published by Start2Finish Books
PO Box 680, Bowie, Texas 76230
www.start2finish.org

Cover Design: Josh Feit, Evangela.com

Unless otherwise noted, all Scripture quotations are from The Holy Bible, English Standard Version®, copyright © 2001 by Crossway Bibles, a publishing ministry of Good News Publishers. Used by permission. All rights reserved. Scripture quotations marked NIV are from HOLY BIBLE, NEW INTERNATIONAL VERSION®. Copyright © 1973, 1978, 1984 by International Bible Society. Used by permission of Zondervan Publishing House. Scripture quotations marked NKJV are from the *New King James Version*. Copyright © 1979, 1980, 1982 by Thomas Nelson, Inc. Used by permission. All rights reserved.

To my dad, Danny, and my mom, Karen:
heroes of the faith that have moved every mountain.

In good times and bad, you have followed
the King and have cherished His church.

This book I devote to you.
I will love you forever and always.

CONTENTS

1

THE ROCKIES OF FAITH

The chocolate cigars have been packed with joy and delivered with love, ready to be "lit" by excited young parents. Balloons are swaying in the waiting room like banners in the breeze. Family is gathered. Cameras are charged. Phones are ready to be dialed. Everyone will soon know that new life has arrived.

The double-doors open, and the "hero" in shining scrubs exits his medical castle. He pulls off his cap, sits down in the chair, and proceeds to fulfill the worst duty of his profession. He looks at this family of faith and tells them, "I'm sorry, but the baby was stillborn. You won't be taking him home today. You won't be taking him home tomorrow. You won't be taking him home at all." The baby will return to the dust from which it came.

Chocolate cigars melt like the tears splashing on the floor.

Balloons are popped by pins of agony.

Shouts of anger and sadness echo through the halls.

The gathered family now disperses to its own respective corner, searching for the words to say.

Cameras aren't used.

Phones aren't dialed.

New life never arrived—only death, and right on schedule. The family of faith wonders why they should continue being faithful.

* * *

Middle-aged "empty-nesters" line their porch and driveway with American flags. They stand proud with other American parents who have graciously allowed their children to defend the freedoms of millions of Americans. They know their offspring face danger every day, but the fight is worth America's cause.

It's 3:00 on a Saturday afternoon. Dad is sitting in his recliner, watching the pigskin cross the end zone. Mom is on the porch, reading the latest edition of the most popular magazine, drinking her coffee in the coolness of the autumn day.

The phone rings in the kitchen. Naturally, dad doesn't get up because it's the fourth quarter, and that would break all laws of couch-potato etiquette. Mom puts down her magazine, runs into the kitchen with coffee in hand, and answers the phone on the fourth ring. How nice it would be to hear her son's voice.

It has been months now. A few emails were sent back and forth, but nothing substitutes the sound of "I love you, Mom" from the voice of your child.

Mom doesn't hear his voice.

In fact, she won't hear it again in this life—only in the life to come. Her son's body is cruising at 32,000 feet, being transported back to the mainland, draped in the flag of honor.

She will greet him one last time. But this time, he won't respond. Instead of running to her with arms wide open, he will be carried to her with arms crossed over by fellow heroes who defend the stars and the stripes.

Is faith really worth it?

Is this the reward for believing in that which can't be seen— the loss of life by one who had so much left to live?

* * *

A young woman sits at her desk, crunching numbers like a machine. She has been clocking in, clocking out, looking for the pot of gold at the end of the rainbow known as the American dream. She earned the degree. She put in the time. She's gained the experience. Now it's her turn for the corner office, the intern who brings her coffee, and an occasional cruise on the corporate jet.

Everyone in the office knows it's that time of year again—promotion week. Each "robot" sits in its cubicle, waiting to receive its orders, and hopefully, the right to climb the next rung on the ladder.

The sound of Bostonian dress shoes inch closer to the workspace. The boss is coming to award the promotion. The footsteps get closer.

And closer.

And closer.

Is this the day she's been waiting for?

No.

This is the day she has feared.

The promotion is given to the lucky winner in the cubicle next to hers. Yes, the one without the master's degree or the experience. The junior employee on staff. It's the story of her life.

Another missed promotion.

Another missed opportunity.

Another painful reminder that her work isn't noticed, even though she works harder than anyone else on staff.

How do you have faith when nothing pans out the way you planned?

The bills can't be paid.

The children won't obey.

Your wife wants to leave you because you bring nothing worthwhile to the relationship.

Your husband is like a kid in a candy store with other women because you can't lose those nagging twenty pounds.

The friends who said, "Give me a call if I can help," don't pick up the phone when you do.

Your family, who is supposed to love you regardless of the reason, loves you if the "reason" coincides with their schedule.

Do you get my drift?

It's all across the board. It might be as dreadful as a stillborn baby, or as painful as the rejection of friends and family. Life is full of challenges that cripple our faith, and when our faith is crippled, our desire to be faithful follows suit.

When life hands us lemons that lack the juice for lemonade, how do we remain positive? How do we view the glass as half-full? Most of all, how do we remain faithful to a faithful God, when our faith wants to waver like feathers blowing in the wind? That's why I've written this book.

Grab a cup of your favorite coffee and let's begin this journey together. But before we do, let's seek guidance from our Navigator, the only One who knows every hair on your head and mine. Please join me in this prayer.

Our Great and Eternal God, we thank you for your constant grace and mercy that flows into our lives from your porch in heaven, because of the cross of Calvary that held your Son on its beams. Father, we know as you know that this world is full of many problems, but these problems cannot, and should not, define who we are. Help us, Father, to strive for faith in a very faithless world. Revive our spirit through your Spirit, so we can pursue you through the haze and fog of sin. In the name of Jesus the Savior we pray, Amen.

With every turn of the page, may we grow in the grace and knowledge of Jesus.

FOR REFLECTION

1. As we begin this journey, what thoughts are circling through your mind?

2. What fears do you have?

3. What frustrations do you hold with God?

4. How do you think this book can help you?

5. Are you ready to accept the challenges in this book?

2

EMBRACE WEAKNESS

It was a sunny, beautiful day in Judea. Jesus had just spent a powerful afternoon with Peter, James, and John on a mountain of majesty. He had been transfigured before them. His face shined like the sun. His clothes were white as lightning.

The voice of God echoed from the summit, "This is my beloved Son, with whom I am well pleased; listen to him" (Matthew 17:5)! Even Moses and Elijah appeared on the mountain, representing the spiritual legacy of the Law and the Prophets.

But when Jesus, Peter, James, and John descended from that life-changing experience, a huge crowd surrounded the nine remaining apostles at base camp. A desperate father found Jesus, fell at His feet and said, "Lord, have mercy on my son, for he is an epileptic and he suffers terribly. For often he falls into the fire, and often into the water" (Matthew 17:15).

This father had already begged the apostles for help, but it was a swing and a miss. The apostles tried to heal the boy, but they failed. Though they were equipped with miraculous ability, nothing miraculous was happening.

Jesus was frustrated with the crowd, but even more so with His chosen followers. Their faith wasn't where it needed to be. They still weren't getting it right. So Jesus, a discouraged teacher, cried out to His students, "O faithless and twisted generation, how long am I to be with you? How long am I to bear with you? Bring him here to me" (Matthew 17:17).

A few moments later, Jesus healed the child, the crowd went wild, and they saw the power of God.

But when the "pep rally" was over, the confused apostles pulled Jesus to the side and asked him, "Why couldn't we do that?" After all, Jesus had given them the power months ago. They had been doing it every week, just like professionals. But this time, it was different. They sat defeated as appalled amateurs.

So Jesus illustrated their ignorance, "Because of your little faith. For truly, I say to you, if you have faith like a grain of mustard seed, you will say to this mountain, 'Move from here to there,' and it will move, and nothing will be impossible for you" (Matthew 17:20-21).

It's quite poetic that, as soon Jesus comes down off a mountain, He tells the apostles how to move mountains. It's a verse that makes us feel invincible. With faith even as small as the mustard seed that disappears in the palm of our hand, we can move mountains.

But what happens when, like the apostles, we don't have that faith? What happens when we look at those mountains—the challenges of life hovering over our existence—*and the mountains won't move*? This book strives to answer that question and solve that dilemma.

In each chapter, we will consider ways to survive a struggling faith so our faith can regain the momentum to move the mountains before us.

As we begin our journey together, we consider the first way to strengthen a struggling faith—*Embrace Weakness*.

To confess when we don't have it all together; to admit that regardless or our tenure, we're still amateurs; to convince ourselves that even we—Jesus-following, Bible-believing people—need to return to the basic matters of faith.

There's probably no better example than Paul's thorn in the flesh in 2 Corinthians 12.

Paul had received great revelations about Heaven.

He had heard things he wasn't permitted to tell.

He was caught up to paradise.

And these heavenly visions and sounds plugged Paul's memory in this "out of body" experience with the Lord. Much different than anything you or I have ever experienced. That's probably why Paul wasn't "permitted" to tell us what it was really like (2 Corinthians 12:4).

But as soon as Paul experienced these "confidential" events, he was humbled back to the level of mortal man. That's usually how it goes, isn't it? As soon as we get the "goose bumps," we're reminded that we aren't as great as the greatness we just witnessed.

Enter Paul into the scene. That's exactly what happened to him, so he said there was "given me a thorn in my flesh, a messenger of Satan, to torment me" (2 Corinthians 12:7 NIV).

It's important to note that this painful thorn was *Satan* at work—it wasn't an unjust act of God. God allowed it to happen just like God allowed Job to endure many painful experiences. Just like God allows you to endure painful experiences. Just like God allows me to endure painful experiences, and trust me when I say that I've endured many. Sometimes they were so painful that giving up on God seemed like not only the most desirable option, but also the most reasonable.

Today, I shudder in ministry when Christians ask, "Why is God doing this to me?" I shudder because it's a question I've asked. No, let me re-phrase that. It's a question I *still* ask.

And when I realize that after all of these years of being a Christian I still ask it, I shudder in complete shame.

But each time, I'm reminded that God doesn't do anything to us. He allows things to happen in our lives that test our faith and our endurance of faithfulness. That's exactly why James, the brother of Jesus, writes, "Consider it pure joy, my brothers, whenever you face trials of many kinds, because you know that the testing of your faith develops perseverance" (James 1:2-3 NIV).

However, just because the "testing" occurs, God doesn't hover over the black kettle with pointy hat and wand in hand, dreaming of dilemmas to derail our spiritual growth. These qualities are reserved for the tempter, deceiver, and liar of Hell.

We don't know exactly what Paul's "thorn" was. The word "thorn" means "stake"—Paul says a "stake" was in his flesh, so we know it was physical. Some say it was poor eyesight.

21

Nevertheless, Paul thought that it was affecting his effectiveness as a minister.

So Paul pleaded with God three different times for the thorn to be removed, but each time God came back and said, "No—the thorn will stay—for my grace is sufficient for you. My mercy is enough. Even though it's painful, you can survive."

Isn't it amazing how a "thorn" teaches Paul to embrace the weakness in his life? It was obviously a lesson well learned, because after Jesus says, "My grace is sufficient for you." Paul says, "I will boast all the more gladly about my weaknesses" (2 Corinthians 12:9 NIV).

If you haven't noticed, that's not the status quo. We often "boast" about our strengths. When people ask us, "What experience do you have?" we spout off our accomplishments at the drop of a hat. It seems like some people even sleep with an updated résumé in their back pocket.

When we interview for a job, we're trained to turn our weaknesses into strengths. When the employer asks, "What is your greatest weakness?" we're trained to say, "Oh, I guess my greatest weakness is that I work too hard." What employer will think, "You're too dependable. We can't hire you—we only hire lazy gluttons and bums at this place?"

Yes, we boast about our strengths, but how many people boast about their weaknesses? How many people say, "I've messed up," "I've made mistakes", and "I've failed"? Not many—if any—until they're caught.

And Paul doesn't just say, "I will boast about my weaknesses." He says, "I will boast about them *gladly*" (2 Corinthians 12:9 NIV). Paul wants everyone, you and me included, to know that he will embrace weakness, because when he does, Christ's power rests on him.

That's why the next statement is such a natural response. Paul says, "For when I am weak, then I am strong" (2 Corinthians 12:10 NIV). That's not what the world says—the world says, "When you're weak, you're weak."

You have bad credit? We're not going to approve the loan.

You've been fired? We're not going to hire you.

You've been divorced? You don't understand commitment.

You're weak, and that's the way it's going to be.

Paul has a different perspective. He says, "I don't really want to be strong—I want to be weak, because when I realize how weak I am, that's when God makes me strong." "God chose what is foolish in the world to shame the wise; God chose what is weak in the world to shame the strong" (1 Corinthians 1:27).

Embracing weakness makes mountains move. We might think it would be the other way around, but according to Scripture, that's exactly how it works.

And here's the piece that completes the puzzle: *To embrace weakness, we must admit when we're weak.* That gem is often forgotten, and we understand why. It's not our favorite pass time.

Confessing that we're broken and burdened goes against the grain. But according to God's Word, that's exactly what we should be doing.

Fathers, there's nothing wrong with admitting weakness to your families. That you haven't been the father you need to be. That you made mistakes. That you allowed the workplace to become your happy place. That the stress of life became unbearable. But by the grace of God, daddy will do better. In fact, one day, your children will respect you more than you know because you embraced weakness.

Husbands and wives, it's important that you confess not only to God, but also to each other when you haven't been the spouse God wants you to be. Husbands, that you have failed to love your wife as Christ loved you. Wives, that you have failed to submit to your husband and pay him the proper respect. One day, you will look back, and you might just say that embracing weakness was the life jacket that saved your marriage.

As Christians, it's critical to talk about our faith when it isn't secure. As strong as we might appear on the outside, we're weak on the inside and we need strength. One day, we might look back at our faith journey and realize that embracing weakness was the fuel that kept us traveling.

When my faith struggled, it was amazing to have people offer their ears to listen and shoulders to cry on. In fact, it was the very thing that kept me going.

We desperately need the humility to fall on our knees and say, "Lord, have mercy on us, we are sinners. We have failed you. We dare not try to take one step alone."

Why is that so important? When you embrace weakness, you become strong. Christ's power rests on you. And guess what: Those mountains that won't move begin to move, ever so slowly.

As we close this chapter, ask yourself this question—how much stronger would the church be if the church could, and would, embrace weakness?

It's very easy for us to turn the church into a "club"—a place where we pay our dues so we can "belong," a place where we play by the same rules, a place where we dress the same, look the same, believe the same, and live the same.

Now, don't get me wrong. It's not a bad thing to be a close-knit group of people. That's one of the many things that make the church so special. But the church isn't a club; the church is a clinic.

Just think about an environment where…

You can openly confess your mistakes without ridicule.

You can pull off the mask and be who you really are.

You can say, "I'm broken," and when the words leave your mouth, others surround you, hug you, love you, and say, "We're broken too. Let's heal together."

Don't dream about people like that—*be* people like that. Don't imagine an environment like that—*make* an environment like that. I believe it's possible—not only possible, but also mandatory.

The gourmet "feast" officially begins with Paul's recipe, "Therefore I will boast all the more gladly about my weaknesses, so that Christ's power may rest on me" (2 Corinthians 12:9 NIV).

Are you weak? I am too. Let's boast together.

FOR REFLECTION

1. In what areas are you strong?

2. In what areas are you weak?

3. How do you differentiate between the two?

4. If God makes His power perfect in weakness, has God made you perfect? How do you know?

5. What types of things keep that from happening?

6. What is it about weakness that scares us?

7. What is it about strength that makes us arrogant?

8. Besides the Lord, whom can you confess weakness to? Seek out such an individual.

9. Who can use you as their confidant and friend for the same reason? Make yourself approachable to such individuals.

3

COUNT YOUR BLESSINGS

We have begun a journey entitled, *When Mountains Won't Move: How to Survive a Struggling Faith.* This idea stems from Matthew 17. When Jesus came down from the Mount of Transfiguration, a father fell at Jesus' feet begging Him to heal his son who was suffering from seizures. The disciples had tried to heal the boy while Jesus was on the mountain, but they couldn't do it.

Now Jesus had arrived, so the father was pleading with the One who could perform the miracle.

Sure enough, Jesus healed the child, and everyone was impressed. After the healing, the apostles wanted to know why they couldn't heal the boy, so Jesus gave that heart-wrenching answer, "Because you have so little faith—if your faith was stronger, even as small as mustard seed—you could move mountains" (Matthew 17:20).

Jesus descends from the mountain and He tells us how to move mountains. But sometimes, our faith is smaller than a mustard seed. Sometimes the mountains won't move. When that happens, how do we survive?

* * *

In the last chapter, we said that the first thing we need to do is Embrace Weakness. Like the apostle Paul, we need to boast about our weaknesses so Christ's power will rest on us. When we admit that we don't have it all together, Christ mends our broken lives. In this chapter, we will discuss the second way to move mountains—*Count Your Blessings*.

Counting blessings is a difficult task. For example, what exactly is a "blessing"? Are some things blessings, or just happenstance? How do we know when something appears to be a blessing but is really just a curse?

Sometimes, when we count our blessings, the spiritual arithmetic doesn't always work. In times of trouble, we don't compute our blessings very quickly.

As a child, when I was already irritable, there was nothing more irritating than my mother telling me to count my blessings. I didn't want to count my blessings. I wanted to count my burdens. Adults are the same way. But the author of Psalm 100 helps us simplify the task by giving us special strategies.

There's a good chance you're very familiar with this beautiful Psalm. You might have even memorized it as a child. It's unique in many ways.

We see the religious devotion of the Jews when the psalmist writes in v. 4, "Enter his gates with thanksgiving, and his courts with praise! Give thanks to him; bless his name!" What an experience it would have been to enter the gates of the temple, to stand in the courtyards of that monstrosity and praise God!

* * *

We see how we're supposed to worship in vv. 1-2, "Shout for joy to the Lord, all the earth. Worship the Lord with gladness; come before him with joyful songs" (NIV). Our worship should be celebratory—it should be fun and exciting. God is glad, and we must imitate His gladness.

31

One day, a man was visiting a church with his wife on vacation. The preacher said something riveting and inspirational, so the man shouted, "Praise the Lord!" The woman in the pew in front of him turned around with a stern face and said, "We don't do that here!"

You know what she meant.

I know what she meant.

She wasn't saying that they didn't praise God; just that they didn't want to get carried away in the process.

For this woman (and many worshippers), crossing the reverence ravine borders on the city limits of blasphemy. I understand why worshippers must be candidly cautious in worship, but a refusal to be excited about God can be interpreted as a refusal to praise God.

The psalmist says, "Shout for joy ... all the earth!" It's something everyone should do—every color, nation, tribe, and age. But let's dive deeper into Psalm 100 and view it from a different angle—how it can teach us to count our blessings.

* * *

"Know that the LORD, he is God! It is he who made us, and we are his; we are his people, and the sheep of his pasture" (v. 3). Zoom in on the first idea—"It is he who made us, and we are his." The God who created the earth that operates on four beautiful seasons, that sits perfectly in the solar system, and that provides air for us to breathe and food for us to eat—that God created us.

And He didn't just create us. Scripture says we're "fearfully and wonderfully made" (Psalm 139:14 NIV). The human body is an amazing machine that doesn't need a warranty or owner's manual. The human mind has more memory than modern computers. The human heart has more power than the strongest batteries. Other translations phrase it this way, "It is He who has made us, and not we ourselves" (Psalm 100:3 NKJV).

I really appreciate that wording. Hollywood says we can make ourselves. Actors live and die by the hand of the plastic surgeon. If they don't like their appearance, no problem—they pay surgeons thousands of dollars, and the face that they don't like can look like someone's that they do like (which, by the way, is a face that someone else can't stand).

If you don't believe me, who do you think is the most attractive person in Hollywood? Who do you think is the most unattractive person in Hollywood? Are you surprised that you can answer both questions? I'm not. You shouldn't be either. Everyone can answer because everyone plays the silly game.

But God's perspective is very different. He designed us in His image (Genesis 1:26); if we don't like the way we look, we really don't like the way God looks. We might choose to lose weight or gain muscle to be healthier. We might change our hair color to look younger or trendier. But overall, our body was created by the hands of God, and when the world says we don't look "good," God says, "You look grand, and I wouldn't have it any other way. You look like me."

Teenage America desperately needs to absorb this message. They listen to the lies of the world that tell them to be skinnier. They hear the definition of what it means to be "beautiful," but society's prototype differs drastically from God's. Movie and music stars destroy years of hard earned reputation for a few minutes on the biggest stage. I have to believe that God shakes His head and says, "I like you just the way you are because I made you."

The psalmist goes onto to say in that same verse, "We are his people, and the sheep of his pasture." It doesn't matter how old we are; we want to belong. It hurts when we aren't picked for the team. It stings when we don't receive the invitation. We start to feel like outsiders with nothing or no one to claim as ours.

But God says, "You do belong. You belong to Me. You're sheep in My pasture—you're a special herd". That's why Jesus picks up the torch and says in John 10:14-15, "I am the Good Shepherd—the sheep know Me, I know My sheep—I even lay down My life for them. They will always be My sheep as long as they stay in My pasture." We belong to Jesus. Jesus belongs to us. There's no greater blessing than that.

* * *

"For the LORD is good; his steadfast love endures forever, and his faithfulness to all generations" (Psalm 100:5).

The "Lord is good"—what exactly does that mean?

Is the Lord "good" like your favorite fried chicken? Is the Lord "good" like a winning sports team? Is the Lord "good" like a dependable product?

Many Hebrew words for "good" appear in the Old Testament, but this word appears 33 times. It's a word that discusses the inherent nature of God, but it's also a word that means "benevolent"—the One who has all (God) gives to those who have little (us).

Stress clouds our vision, but God is very benevolent. He gives us numerous material blessings that we simply fail to acknowledge. Sometimes it's fortune; sometimes it's our "daily bread" (Matthew 6:11). Either way, when we look back we can see and say that God took care of us. You know why? He is good. He is benevolent.

Do you have food to eat? Clothes to wear? Do you know where you will spend the night? If you answered "yes" to even one of those questions, God has been very good to you.

God never promised us wealth. He promised us blessing, and blessing isn't solely measured by a bank balance. If you think that God promised you wealth, you think that God promised you something His own Son didn't even experience.

Is it acceptable and honorable to be wealthy? Sure. Men like Abraham and David had great wealth, but that wealth didn't define their story. Their story was defined by blessing.

So is yours.

So is mine.

That's exactly why Jesus says, "Don't worry about tomorrow—what you will eat, what you will wear—for if God takes care of the sparrow, He will take care of you" (Matthew 6: 25-30). We have clothes on our backs. We plan to eat in a few hours (You're probably thinking about it now). God has been "good" to us.

* * *

The psalmist says, "His steadfast love endures forever."

Love's longevity is foreign in our world. The divorce rate has skyrocketed to unseen heights, even in the church. And most divorced couples say they hired attorneys because they fell out of love.

Last year, the San Antonio news provided a fascinating video. A local police detective went undercover, pretending to be a well-known hit man in the area. Everything was caught on tape. They were sitting in this woman's car as she made the request to terminate her husband. They even negotiated a price, location, and time. At the end of the conversation, this detective, pretending to be the murder specialist asked her, "Why are you doing this? " She answered, "Well, I've fallen out of love, but I still care about him. I didn't want to drag him through a painful divorce, so I thought I would just handle it this way."

How thoughtful. She didn't want to divorce him, so she thought she would just have him killed. Much better.

Love fails with people, but love never fails with God—His love endures forever. He loved us before we were born. He will love us after we die. And day by day, God's love keeps us strong. That's the truth of our Father. That's the medicine that helps us sleep in peace even in the strongest storms. Forget the Nyquil. Listen to God's promise. It's real.

* * *

Finally, the psalmist says, "His faithfulness continues through all generations" (NIV).

Parents agonize about leaving their children something valuable after they're gone. Maybe it's a trust fund. Maybe it's a life insurance policy, property, stocks, or bonds.

Don't get me wrong—that's important and special, but parents don't have to carry the entire burden. They don't have to obsess over leaving their children tangible value. God has already left the perfect gift—"His faithfulness continues through all generations."

In the same way God made us, God made our children. In the same way God has been good to us, God will be good to them. In the same way God loves us forever, God will love them forever. His faithfulness is an eternal flame that continues to blaze.

We can choose not to count our blessings. We have that right, but it's not wise. Psalm 100 provides a lifetime of thankfulness. We serve a God who made us with His own hands. When the world says that we're useless, God says that we're flawless. When the world closes the door, God keeps it open. We serve a God who is "good"—a God who gives material blessings, big and small. We serve a God who loves forever, even when people can't love us for days. We serve a God whose faithfulness continues through all generations. When everything changes, God never will.

And if we can't count our blessings, we will never move mountains because, eventually, if we don't count our blessings, *our blessings won't count us.*

On the Day of Judgment, God will look into a sea of faces that He has blessed—faces from every tribe, nation, and century. But just because we're blessed in this life, we have no guarantee that we'll be blessed in the life to come. It's only those who count their blessings on earth that will be counted on the Day of Judgment. That's when the guarantee is granted.

When this passing world is done, God will know who counted their blessings and who didn't. Your appreciation will be remembered like the sun remembers its schedule.

Many years ago, a missionary went to the island of Tobago. For weeks, his team built homes and dug wells. They even performed medical missions. But on the last day of the mission trip, a woman who had suffered from leprosy her entire life—who had been an outcast by society for decades—who had never experienced the love and fellowship of Christians—cautiously walked into their worship. For the first time in her life, she stared at the crowd face-to-face rather than turning away in shame. Her nose and ears were completely eroded from leprosy, but she lifted her fingerless hand in the air and asked, "Can we please sing the song, 'Count your many blessings?'"

A story like that encourages me about how far I've come, but it also reminds me of how far I have to go. When the mountains won't move, it's easy to get down in the dumps. From time to time, we all wallow in the filth of our own failing faith.

But counting burdens rather than blessings never solves the problem. And when we think about a dying leper counting her blessings, it should change the way we "count" forever.

God loves the melody of an appreciative heart. When He hears it, He strengthens struggling faith, and the mountains always move.

Count your blessings, name them one by one, and it will surprise you what the Lord has done.

FOR REFLECTION

1. Take a sheet of paper. On one side, write down the burdens in your life. On the other side, write down the blessings. After a few minutes of doing this, which list is longer?

2. Why do you think this list is longer? Why do you think the other list is shorter?

3. Read Genesis 12:1-3. Diagnose the three stages of blessings.

4. Have you experienced all three stages? Why or why not?

5. How can you be more thankful?

6. How can you be less entitled?

7. How will people know the difference between your thankfulness and entitlement?

4

IMPROVE YOUR SERVE

J esus said if we have faith as small as a mustard seed, we can look at the mountains in the distance, say, "Move from here to there," and they will. But in our darkest days, the mountains sometimes won't move, and when they don't, it causes great emotional pain.

I want do something a little bit different as we begin this chapter together. We're going to take two quizzes. Grab a piece of paper and take your time answering these questions. Have your friends do the same and see what happens.

QUIZ #1

1. Name the five richest people in America.
2. Name the last five Heisman Trophy winners.

3. Name five Nobel Prize winners.
4. Name the last five Super Bowl champions.

QUIZ #2

1. Name your five favorite teachers.
2. Name five friends you can always call.
3. Name five people who prayed for you.
4. Name five people who loved your children.

Which quiz was easier?

I may not know your entire life story. I may not know every challenge you've faced or victory you've won. But I do know who influenced you the most in your life—someone who served you. We always remember those who went out of their way to make a difference in our lives.

That's the theme for this chapter. When mountains won't move, *Improve your Serve.*

One of the greatest servants in the Bible is found in Joshua 2, the woman named Rahab. Her story begins with the entrance of the two spies. Joshua had been formally chosen as the new leader of Israel, and one of his first moves as captain was to send two spies into Jericho to canvas the land.

It's interesting that Joshua sent spies. God didn't tell him to do it. No one asked him to do it. But he did it anyway.

When we think critically about Joshua and his past, I think we know why he did. Joshua was one of the two brave spies that went into the land of Canaan forty years before and said that it was possible to conquer it. Joshua and Caleb came back and said, "We can take the land", but the others said that they were like grasshoppers standing before giants (Numbers 13:33). Consequently, Israel spent forty years in the wilderness, one year for every day the spies were in the land, because ten cowards didn't trust God.

So years later, this righteous spy turned righteous leader sent two unnamed spies into Jericho from Shittim. Shittim was about five miles east of the Jordan River, and the Jordan was about five miles east of Jericho. It was a full day's trip on foot. When these two spies arrived in Jericho, they immediately hid in the home of Rahab.

Now why did they go to Rahab's home? Rahab was a prostitute in the city of Jericho. Some translations say that she was an "Inn Keeper", but that's not exactly right. That gives her too much credit. When she is referenced in the New Testament, the Greek word *pornē* is used to describe her life—the same word that gave us the English word "pornography." Yes, people of antiquity were light years ahead of us when it came to sexual sin. We developed the website. They developed the house site. You could live and breathe infidelity then, just like you can now.

The spies' plan was genius. They weren't there to satisfy their lust but to save their lives. If two random men walked into the home of a well-known prostitute, it wouldn't cause any suspicion. No one would notice. Men did this daily. This was Rahab's bread and butter—literally.

But when the king heard that two strangers were at Rahab's home, he told Rahab to disclose who they were. She told the king's messengers that the spies had already left, and so the messengers set out toward the Jordan River to find them—back towards Shittim. All the while, Rahab hid the spies on the roof. Why did this prostitute go to such great efforts to help these two men she didn't even know?

As the story progresses, once again, we begin to understand why. Rahab begins conversing with the spies. Rahab, a Gentile woman, begins the conversation by saying, "I know that the LORD has given you the land" (Joshua 2:9). How did she know? She wasn't an Israelite—she didn't know Moses or Joshua. How could she make such claims? She tells us why.

She heard about Israel crossing the Red Sea on dry ground. She heard what happened to the two kings who lost their lives because they picked up the sword and tried to engage the nation of God in battle.

* * *

It's amazing that the very first confession of God's power in the book of Joshua comes from an unbelieving prostitute. That explains why Jesus told the Pharisees in Matthew 21:31, "Tax collectors and the prostitutes go into the kingdom of God before you." But with passion, Rahab tells these two spies, "When we heard of it, our hearts melted and everyone's courage failed because of you, for the LORD your God is God in heaven above and on the earth below" (Joshua 2:11 NIV).

But then this conversing turns into a contract. Rahab realizes who she's talking to, the spies of Yahweh, so she says, "Please swear to me by the LORD that, as I have dealt kindly with you, you also will deal kindly with my father's house, and give me a sure sign that you will save alive my father and mother, my brothers and sisters, and all who belong to them, and deliver our lives from death" (Joshua 2:12-13).

The spies were touched by Rahab's faith, but even more by her servant's heart. So they said, "Our lives for your lives" (Joshua 2:14 NIV). In other words, if you take care of us, we will take care of you.

However, there were some conditions attached to the contract. The spies said, "When God brings us in to destroy this great city of Jericho, you must hang this scarlet cord out your window—that will be the sign that we still have an agreement." And, "All of your relatives, parents, siblings, they must stay in your home when we come—if they go out into the streets, we can't protect them." And finally, "All of this must be kept as our secret" (Joshua 2:17-20).

Rahab agreed, which led to the deliverance of the spies. She lowered the men down the wall with a rope. She told the spies to run for the mountains (of all places) and to hide for three days. Rahab knew how to create the distraction. She sent them to the mountains. And then, based on her contract, she tied the scarlet cord in her window.

Eventually, the two spies made it back to Joshua and said, "Let us march—the Lord has given the whole land into our hands" (Joshua 2:24). They marched.

And God conquered.

It's one of the Bible's greatest stories, but it's also a perfect picture of our journey. *A servant's heart made Rahab's faith real.* Think about it—she knew that God existed, even before these two spies entered into her home. She believed because of the Exodus, which happened four decades before. She believed because of the demise of kings Sihon and Og. But her beliefs didn't change her life style—she was still a prostitute.

But when Rahab became a servant, her faith that had been hiding in darkness burst onto the stage of light. She risked her life helping men she didn't even know, and for the first time in Rahab's heartbreaking life, the mountains moved.

Today, Rahab's legacy lives on in Scripture. The writer of Hebrews includes her in the Heroes of Faith, even though her life wasn't always faithful (Hebrews 11:31). James uses her as evidence that faith without deeds is useless (James 2:25).

Even when we study biblical ancestry, we see the depth of Rahab's influence. Rahab married a man named Salmon, who many scholars think was possibly one of the two spies in Joshua 2.

Salmon and Rahab had a son named Boaz. Boaz married Ruth. Rahab understood the importance of serving and loving others. It's obvious that this virtue was passed to her son Boaz, who married Ruth, an outsider, whose family had turned on her for leaving Moab. Ruth was brought into the covenant with God, riding on the coat tails of Boaz. Boaz had a heart for people just like his mother. Even Jesus, the greatest servant of all, descended from Rahab's bloodline.

And it's not just Rahab—*it's the servant heart that makes our faith real as well.* Jesus never appeared more divine than in the Upper Room on the night of His death. For three years, He had been performing miracles, teaching with authority, and bringing peace to hostile situations. But when He bent down, picked up the towel, and washed feet, He proved the full extent of His godliness.

And Jesus hands us the towel to do the same.

We can all improve our serve. We might do something bold. We might serve in ways where others haven't served before. A Master washing feet was cutting edge. A prostitute providing protection was history in the making.

Maybe we develop our own ministry. Our service doesn't have to be bold—it can be simple like mowing a yard, writing a note, or lending a hand. Sometimes the menial task means the most. But if you feel like your faith is struggling, ask yourself this question—when was the last time that I served *someone else*?

When we improve our serve, our serve improves us. We become the hands and the feet of Jesus. We pick up the towel. We lower the rope. And mountains move.

* * *

When I was in sixth grade, I went to Arlington, Texas with my youth group on a mission trip to paint houses. If you're a sports fan, you're familiar with Arlington, Texas. Arlington houses two major stadiums—the baseball stadium for the Texas Rangers and the football stadium for the Dallas Cowboys. Even though Arlington has some very prominent areas, it is also the home of some impoverished neighborhoods. In the summer of 1999, our group went deep into the projects to the home of a man named Mr. Pheres.

Mr. Pheres was a retired painter. Needless to say, he wasn't too impressed with our junior high painting skills. Have you ever seen a bunch of pre-teens paint a house? And paint it baby blue, of all colors? It's a nightmare. They get paint on everything, except what they're supposed to be painting. There was one boy in our group who got paint in his underwear every day. How do you pull that one off? Paint in your underwear? Incredible.

The first day of the extravaganza, Mr. Pheres avoided us like the plague because he couldn't bear the sight of our disaster destroying his home. The second day, he put drop cloths down on every inch of his property—even in the grass—as we were quickly turning his green Bermuda into Kentucky "baby blue."

But on the third day, when we hung a new mailbox on his front porch that we had bought with our own money (mainly because we couldn't get the paint off the old one), Mr. Pheres was a different man. As we gathered together in a circle and sang to him "We love you with the love of the Lord," tears began to fall from that stone cold face. The scorn turned into a smile. The hands that wouldn't shake ours grazed our backs as he hugged each novice painter.

I'm convinced to this day that on that hot summer afternoon in Arlington, Texas in 1999, Mr. Pheres didn't see a single drop of spilled paint. He saw a product of love painted by us but perfected by Jesus. As we climbed into the church vans to ride off into the sunset, he even told us that it was the best paint job he had ever seen.

We came back to visit Mr. Pheres in December. That was part of the plan for our mission trip—we painted houses in

June, and followed up in December by bringing cookies and singing Christmas carols to the family.

But when we entered his living room, we had no clue how life-changing the following conversation would be. We discovered that Mr. Pheres had become Brother Pheres. He had been immersed into the blood of Jesus just a few weeks before.

His sins had been washed away. He had received the gift of the Holy Spirit. He had entered the Kingdom of God. And with tears in his eyes, he began to tell us why.

> I've heard a lot of sermons in my day. For 80 years, people and preachers have visited my house, begging me to come to church. I've read books. I've been to the seminars. I've even been to the potlucks. But I never believed it, and I never understood why, until I met you kids. When you painted my house, on your own time, with your own money, I finally saw the love of Jesus.
>
> — Brother Pheres
> *December 1999*

As I write this story—one that I've told hundreds of times—my spine still chills, and my eyes still tear. God used something as simple as a paintbrush to save a soul. And the mountains that had blocked Mr. Pheres' reception to Jesus for decades finally moved.

That isn't a story about me—that's a story about you. That's a story about the church. That's a story about God's people and the power that they possess through service. When we serve, Christianity is at its best. Jesus told us it would be that way when He said, "The greatest among you shall be your servant" (Matthew 23:11).

If you want to be great—

Throw the cord out the window.

Pick up the towel.

Stroke a paintbrush.

Do whatever you can to make a difference, and those mountains will move every time. I guarantee it.

FOR REFLECTION

1. As we saw with the quizzes at the beginning of the chapter, when we think about people we have known in our lives, servants rise to the top of our favorites. Who came to your mind first? Why?

2. Have you ever experienced a special, spiritual moment after serving someone else? Why was that moment so special?

3. In what ways can you better serve your church family?

4. In what ways can you better serve your community?

5. How will these ways be similar, but also different?

6. When you think about the people in your life, who needs to be served the most? Why?

7. How will you serve them this week?

8. Most likely, many more "Mr. Pheres" are in our midst, but we don't even realize it. How can you encourage your church family to pursue these people with greater passion and purpose? How can you do the same?

5

RE-PLANT THE SEED

A struggling faith is a fact of life. It comes in different ways, at different times, for different reasons, but it still comes. So far, we've considered ways to help a struggling faith.

We should Embrace Weakness.

We should Count our Blessings.

We should Improve Our Serve.

In this chapter, we will consider the next method to moving mountains—*Re-Plant the Seed*.

Jesus said that if we have faith as small as a mustard seed, we can move mountains. But sometimes our faith isn't even that big—it's smaller than the seed that disappears in our hand. There are many reasons for this struggle, but one of the biggest reasons is that our faith has been planted in the wrong soil.

In Mark 4, Jesus tells a parable about a farmer sowing seed. I don't know much about farming and planting seeds. The only thing I know how to plant is a golf ball in a sand trap, but I do know that Jesus' parable shows us how to re-plant the seed in the right soil.

At this time, Jesus' popularity was increasing. People came from all over to hear what He had to say. On this day, so many came that Jesus had to get in a boat so He could be seen. And so, Jesus tells the parable. He begins by saying, "A farmer went out to sow his seed" (Mark 4:3 NIV).

Who was this farmer? We could say teachers or preachers. Parables can have different meanings and interpretations. But when we look at the context of this parable, we realize that God is the farmer—God sows the seed, the Word of God, all over the earth.

And Jesus mentions the different places where the seed settles. He said, "some seed fell along the path" (Mark 4:4). The path isn't a terrible place to land—it has fairly good conditions, the temperature is about right, and it has access to the sunlight. But it can't grow because birds come along and eat it up.

Then He said, "Other seed fell on rocky ground" (Mark 4:5). Since it was rocky, there wasn't much soil. In the rocks, the seed could grow, but when the sun came out, it would scorch the seed because there was no nourishment.

Then Jesus said, "Other seed fell among thorns" (Mark 4:7). Like the seed in the rocks, it began to grow. But before it reached maturity and stability, it was choked by the bristles and thistles surrounding it.

Finally, Jesus said, "Other seeds fell into good soil" (Mark 4.8). The good soil had everything the other seed was missing. It was rooted, it was nourished, it grew, and it multiplied—not just a little, but up to 30, 60, even 100 times. Jesus offered the conclusion to the sermon when He said, "He who has ears to hear, let him hear" (Mark 4:9).

The people heard. But they didn't truly understand.

* * *

Once the crowd dispersed, the apostles asked, "What do all of these things mean?" He says, "To you has been given the secret of the kingdom of God" (Mark 4:11).

He had chosen them to be His twelve special students, and He would teach them all kinds of spiritual things. But Jesus reminded them, "Everyone else—those who haven't been hand selected—they don't understand, so I speak to them in these stories called 'parables.' Because these people…they see, but they don't accept it. They hear, but they don't want to listen. So hopefully, through these earthly stories with a heavenly meaning, they will understand."

Jesus realized that He wasn't breaking through the dense minds of the apostles, so He asked them, "Do you not understand?" (Mark 4:13). They obviously didn't, or they wouldn't be asking the question.

I can see Jesus shaking His head and saying to them, "If you don't understand this parable, you can't understand any parable—they all relate to this message in one way or another." Realizing what He was up against, Jesus clarified the meaning.

The seed the farmer sows is the Word of God. The different soil refers to the different types of people who hear the Word of God.

Some are like the seed along the path. They hear the Word of God. They're excited about its message. But before they know it, Satan comes along and snatches it right out of their lives (Mark 4:15).

Some are like the seed on the rocks. They hear the word of God. They're filled with joy. They want to be better. But they can't be better because they aren't nourished, and they fall away when the tough times come (Mark 4:16).

Some are like the seed among the thorns. They hear the Word of God, they know what they need to do, and they do it. But worry controls their lives and chokes their ability to be faithful (Mark 4:18).

And some people—"They're like the seed on the good soil" (Mark 4:20). They hear the Word of God, they dwell on its power, and they live by it. Most importantly, they encourage others to do the same.

Jesus broke it down to the nuts and bolts. His message was crystal clear. It takes more than hearing the Word of God. It takes more than opening our hearts to the seed that is scattered. The Word of God must be planted in our lives in the right soil so we can grow the right way.

For years, I thought the different types of soil described the different people in the world, and I think it does because Jesus is speaking to those who hadn't fully accepted Christianity. But the soil also describes the church, and when we look at it that way, it cuts us even deeper.

In the church, some live on the *path*. They hear the Word of God, but Satan steals it from their lives. He may not do it overnight—it's a slow process—but it still happens, and all too often. It happens when the Word of God is no longer taught in the home. Parents expect the church to raise their children. Parents expect Bible school teachers to teach their children. And so the children hear the Word of God at church, but before they make it home, Satan steals it from their memory because the parents never take the rein of responsibility. Consequently, the church raises a generation that is biblically illiterate.

It's not just that way with children; it's also that way with adults. We come to worship. We go to Bible class. We read Scripture. We hear a message from God's Word, and we say, "That's how we need to live."

But at Sunday lunch, we enjoy a meal of Fried Preacher or Sautéed Worship Leader, and we miss the entire purpose of our praise to God. We gossip about people at church. We're rude to our waiter. What happened? We heard the word of God, but Satan stole it from our hearts.

In the church, some live on the *rocks*. They hear the Word with joy, but because they have no root, they quickly die off. These are the people who answer questions in Bible class. They sing in worship. They appear to be really spiritual. But when they go home, they never open the Word, so they don't hear it again until the next Sunday. These people are on fire for God until trouble comes. They lose their job or their spouse, or become sick, and all of a sudden, it's God's fault. He's no longer the hero, but the villain.

These are the college students who leave home to pursue higher education. They've grown up in the church, but unfortunately, they've only grown up with their parents' faith. So when they're on their own, they don't have a faith to sustain them. They can't be nourished by someone else's seed, so they aren't "nourished" at all.

In the church, some live among the *thorns*. They know what they need to do and they begin to do it, but the worries of the world "choke" their success. It's not because they don't know what the Word says—they know exactly what it says. The problem is that they have no sense of priority. Rather than focusing on their citizenship in heaven, they're obsessed with their citizenship on earth—carrying a certain image, being the fastest, the strongest, the richest, and the smartest. And after a while, they're choked by the fleeting images of this world because they realize they can't do enough to impress this world. Once again, there was nothing left to sustain them.

But some in the church live in the good soil.

These people hear the Word of God because they make an effort to assemble with God's people. They study as a family at home. And after they hear the word, they put it into practice. They don't worry so much about being analysts, but activists. That was the problem with the Pharisees. They lectured the Word of God, but they didn't live the Word of God. That's why Jesus told people, "Do as they say, not as they do."

The minority (good soil) does what the majority doesn't do. They produce a crop. They become evangelistic. They spread the seed. They bring others into the fold. And why is that soil so "good"? Because *it's the soil that saves.*

* * *

When the mountains won't move, we must re-plant the seed. God's people have spent too much time on the path, on the rocks, or among the thorns. We need to be in the good soil because when we are, we're strengthened by the power of God.

As we close this chapter, there's one thing we must all remember about this parable: We will all take turns being the farmer. We will scatter the Word of God to our children, our family, and our friends. Sometimes intentionally; sometimes unintentionally. But guess how they will grow? By the soil from which we came.

If we're on the path, they will be on the path.

If we're on the rocks, they will be on the rocks.

If we're among the thorns, they will be among the thorns.

If we're on the good soil, they will be on the good soil.

They will learn from our example.

Which soil are you?

FOR REFLECTION

1. For the majority of your life, which soil have you called "home"?

2. In which soil are you currently living? How do you know?

3. Is it possible to move from soil to soil several times? Why or why not?

4. When you moved soils, how (or when) did you know the move had been made?

5. Take a sheet of paper and make four columns. In your own words, write down different characteristics of living in each soil.

6. Once you have written down the characteristics, mark those that are easiest to overcome. Hardest? Most urgent?

7. Take another sheet of paper. Write down which soil you think you're currently living in. Then ask your spouse or a close friend to give the same evaluation of your life.

8. If the answers differed, answer these two questions: Why did they differ? Which person is right?

9. In one sentence, write down in your own words the main point of Jesus' parable.

10. How will this parable affect your life beginning today?

6

TURN TO THE CHURCH

The journey of faith is full of twists and turns, ups and downs. Even Jesus, after He was baptized, spent forty days in the wilderness being tempted by Satan. If we don't experience challenges in our faith, we probably aren't faithful enough.

When we're challenged, we can turn to money, friends, or hobbies—but there's no greater blessing than *Turning to the Church*.

That's why the author of Hebrews wrote, "Let us not give up meeting together, as some are in the habit of doing, but let us encourage one another—and all the more as you see the Day approaching" (Hebrews 10:25 NIV).

It's the famous church attendance verse that reminds us that we should never forsake the assembly. I certainly think that's an appropriate way to interpret it. As God's people, we need to make an effort to assemble in God's house.

But as we continue our study of moving mountains, let's look at Hebrews 10:25 in a different way—not as a recipe for attendance, but as a necessity for survival.

Hebrews 10:19-24 lists so many benefits that we receive in the Lord's Church. In vv. 19-20, we see that the church has tremendous confidence. The writer says we can "…enter the Most Holy Place" (Hebrews 10:19 NIV).

In the Old Testament, the Most Holy Place (or the Holy of Holies) was the place where only the High Priest could enter, and even then, only once a year. But now as Christians, we have the confidence to enter the new Most Holy Place, heaven. And the reason we have this confidence is because of Jesus.

The writer says He opened a "new and living way" (Hebrews 10:20), a way never seen before. He opened it up through His own body. Through His death, Jesus tore down the veil that kept people from approaching God. Now He serves as the High Priest over the house of God, the church, and we get to serve Him as He serves us.

Since we have that confidence, v. 22 says we can draw near to God with sincere hearts. This isn't a game—this isn't superficial or an old, legalistic tradition—it's real. When we worship, we come before a real God, as real people, with real problems. And He still accepts us for who we are. Because of that, we have full assurance of faith.

Did you catch that? When our faith is weak, we can turn to the church and find full assurance. Our heart—the organ that gives life, but also houses evil—is sprinkled to cleanse our conscience the same way that animals' blood was sprinkled on the altar. And our bodies—the agents that actually commit the sin once the heart devises the plan—are washed through Jesus' blood in baptism, which brings us into the Lord's church.

He goes on to say that because we draw near, we can hold "unswervingly" (Hebrews 10:23 NIV) to the hope we profess. "Unswervingly" is a fun word, isn't it? It's a word that means "without wavering, steadfast, immovable." So when our faith does waver, we turn to the church where faith is unwavering.

Finally, because of all of these benefits, we consider how we can "spur" one another on to love and good deeds (Hebrews 10:24 NIV) The word "spur" actually means "provoke." We can "provoke" one another the wrong way. Someone once said, "The only thing that will keep Christians from heaven is the church." Many times, it's our fellow Christ-followers who really know the buttons to push, and unfortunately, they often push them, very similar to the way fathers can "exasperate" or "provoke" their children to anger (Ephesians 6:3).

But if we can provoke one another the wrong way, we can certainly "provoke" one another the right way! If you've been in the church for any time, you know that's true. Sometimes you don't want to come, but when you do come, you leave feeling better.

Early one Sunday morning, a man was lying in bed while his wife was in the bathroom getting ready for worship. The alarm clock would buzz about every seven minutes. But each time, the husband would roll over and lethargically mash the snooze button. With each push of the button, the wife would yell out from the bathroom, "Tom, sweetie, it's time to get up and get ready for church." She obviously wasn't making much headway because Tom hadn't left the comfort of the sheets. Finally, when the alarm clock buzzed one more time, she dropped her curling iron, ran into the bedroom, threw the covers on the floor and said, "Tom, I'm not going to tell you again—get up!" Well, this irritated Tom. He fired back at her and said, "Woman, leave me alone. I don't want to go to church today. Those people are mean and judgmental. I don't like them. They don't like me. Give me just one reason why I have to go to church." She answered, "Tom, you're the preacher!"

Not everyone wants to go to church. Even preachers who make their living preaching don't always want to preach. But don't you always feel better when you go? Don't you always feel a closer connection to God? Don't you always appreciate Jesus more? Of course, you do. It was designed that way.

The church is God's gift to us, even when we may not always enjoy the singing, teaching, preaching, people, or coffee! Sometimes you don't know how you will carry your burden, but the church steps in and carries it with you—that's why Paul says, "Bear one another's burdens" (Galatians 6:2).

When I was preaching in Llano, Texas in my first ministry work, I learned a lesson I'll never forget. One of our Elders was a man by the name of Curtis Osbourn. Curtis was one of the dearest men you could ever hope to meet, as was his wife, Carolyn. I arrived in Llano, Texas in August 2009 as a 22-year-old "kid," ready to preach the gospel. Curtis and Carolyn took my wife and me under their wing.

In August 2009, Carolyn was an icon in the town of Llano. She was the Executive Vice President for Llano National Bank—the biggest bank in town. She and Curtis had raised their children in Llano and owned some land outside the small community. They were known as prominent members of the Llano Church of Christ and as great citizens of Llano, Texas. Everyone wanted to be like Curtis and Carolyn.

In September 2009, Carolyn started complaining about severe headaches. The pain meds weren't working, so she decided to go see a specialist in Austin. After visiting this specialist, doctors discovered that Carolyn was suffering from a stage four brain tumor—the worst kind of brain tumor one could have.

September was headaches. October and November were months of radiation. December was time for family. Then, on a cold morning in January 2010, Carolyn got up in the middle of the night, and as she was walking down the hallway, she collapsed. She was gone. It was all over.

In a little over four months, the Carolyn Osbourn that was as healthy as a horse was laid to rest six feet below.

The memorial service was packed. I received the distinct privilege of speaking about her life. The small funeral home in Llano sat 300 people wall-to-wall, and the service was standing room only. Everyone came to pay their respects for such a fine lady. Her death rocked the entire community. No one could fathom why or how this had happened.

* * *

Fast forward two months to a cool, rainy, spring evening at the Llano Church of Christ in March 2010. Curtis Osbourn was giving the devotional that night for our small church family. Curtis wasn't a public speaker. He hated it. He would rather have been getting a root canal. But that night, he walked with a lighter step and greater confidence.

He opened his Bible, pulled out his notes, and tried to say the things he had prepared. But as tears continued to fall down his face, he folded his notes and placed them back in his Bible. He looked out into the audience with eyes that were grief stricken, yet triggered with hope, and said, "I don't know where I would be tonight without the church." As tears flowed down my cheeks, I sat convicted. I will remember that night forever.

This was an elder, a leader in our church—a "shepherd" telling the "sheep," "I don't know where I would be without you." You don't forget moments like that.

God doesn't forget them either.

In the family of God, when we're spurred toward love and good deeds, we spur others as well. It's a two-way street, and nothing matches that type of power.

When we fully digest the benefits of Hebrews 10:19-24, we appreciate even more the call to action in Hebrews 10:25. When it says, "Let us not give up meeting together," we should say, "Why in the world would we ever give that up?" The writer of Hebrews, speaking on behalf of God, isn't telling us to keep meeting for an attendance quota; he's telling us to keep meeting so we can survive. Sometimes we convince ourselves that God needs us to come. But God doesn't need us; we need Him. Without Him, we're ships lost at sea. But when we walk through the doors of the house of the Lord—

We have confidence that we can enter heaven.

We serve a great High Priest who atones for our every sin.

We have full assurance of faith.

We unswervingly hold onto hope.

Our brothers and sisters spur us on, as we spur them on.

Give up meeting? We would be crazy to do that! With no assembly, there are no benefits. And with no benefits, our faith will always struggle.

Now you know as well as I do that not everyone buys into what I'm saying—not everyone turns to the church because if they did, the church would be bigger than it's ever been. That's obviously not the case.

Some say, "Well, I'm not going to turn to the church because the church is just a big group of hypocrites." One Sunday, a man asked his neighbor to go to church with him. His neighbor said, "I'm not going to church with you—your church is full of hypocrites." The man said, "That's OK, there's always room for one more!"

Being around hypocrites is a part of life. There are hypocrites at school, but you still go to school. There are hypocrites at work, but you still go to work. So if there are hypocrites at church, why wouldn't you still go to church? Does the church not deserve the same forgiveness you give everyone else? Of course, it does.

Some have said, "Sitting in a church makes you a Christian just as much as sitting in a garage makes you a car!" That's partially correct—sitting on a pew doesn't make you a true Christ-follower. But I'll say this—that same car sitting in the garage (even if it doesn't move) is still better than the car sitting outside. Outside there is hail, wind, and bird droppings. At least your car is somewhat protected on the inside, and you immediately know the difference when a car has been garage-kept. Likewise, you can immediately tell the difference between an individual who goes to church and one who doesn't.

Some might even say, "I'm not going to turn to the church because the church never turns to me—it has let me down too many times." If that has happened to you, I am so sorry. That's a real shame. I wish I could go back in time and correct the mistakes that led to your heartache. But let me ask you a real question, and please give yourself a real answer. Do you really think that if you turn to your job, your money, or anything else, you will always find what you need?

Maybe you've tried. Did it work? I guess what I'm trying to say is that the church on its worst day is still better than the world on its best day. It doesn't matter how you paint the picture, we're always better with the church than we are without it.

Do you want to know why I love the church?

I love the church because it's *real*. It's made of real people. It has real problems. But that's OK because we serve a real God.

I love the church because it's a *gift*. We don't deserve it. We don't create it. But by God's grace, we're allowed to enter.

I love the church because it's *stable*. We experience internal challenges that break our hearts. We have external disappointments that bring us to our knees. But even in the hottest debate and darkest conflict, Jesus still says, "I will build my church, and the gates of hell shall not prevail against it" (Matthew 16:18). Businesses close, people die, stocks drop, and trends change, but the church will always be a light on a hill. In case you haven't noticed, Jesus was right.

I love the church because it's *heavenly*. It truly is heaven on earth. When we're assembled, we experience some of the most genuine moments with God and His throne.

And I love the church because it *cares*. During some of the toughest moments in my life, the church has been there to help. And the church will do that for you if you will let it.

That doesn't mean you will always be visited. That doesn't mean you will always be treated like a king or a queen. The church will fail you, but the church will always love you.

Will you love the church in return?

Many people love to talk about what's wrong with the church, but I'm not interested in that conversation. I want to dwell on what's right with the church because so much is. If Jesus died to give it, we can live to love it.

D.L. Moody was a famous evangelist in the 19th century. One cold afternoon, Moody was in Chicago, and he went to the home of the wealthiest man in the city to try and convince him to go to church.

After visiting for about an hour, the cocky businessman looked at Moody and said, "Well, Mr. Moody, I just want you to know that I've been very successful. Look around you. Look at my beautiful home and all of its furnishings. Look at my prestigious clothes and my beautiful books. The church didn't provide any of these things. I did. I don't need the church, and the church doesn't need me."

Moody walked over to the fireplace, took the tongs and pulled out a blazing coal from the fire. As they continued their conversation, that coal turned from orange, to hot, to warm, to cool, to cold, to black, and eventually dead. The object lesson was a thousand times more powerful than any sermon Moody could have preached. The businessman looked at Moody and said, "I'll be at church next Sunday."

When the mountains won't move, turn to the church.

God, through the death of His Son, gave us the church so we wouldn't die. We might think that we'll be just fine without it. But eventually, we'll be that coal that turned from orange, to hot, to cool, to cold, to black, and eventually dead. Don't let the "tongs" pull you away.

Turn to the church.

FOR REFLECTION

1. What is your favorite thing about the church you attend?

2. What is your least favorite thing about the church you attend?

3. This might be painful, but trust the process. Grab a sheet of paper and make two columns. Label one column "Pros" and one column "Cons." Now that you have diagnosed your favorite and least favorite attributes of the church where you attend, try to list the "Pros" and "Cons" the same way in their respective columns. Take ample time to do this.

4. After considering both lists, which is longer? Why do you think that it is?

5. Look at the "Con" list again. Does any reason carry enough credibility to keep you from attending? Why or why not?

6. When you read the words of Hebrews 10:25, "Let us encourage one another," what thoughts come to your mind?

7. If you're dissatisfied with your local church, in what ways can you encourage others?

8. Do you think your encouragement will change your

dissatisfaction? Why or why not?

9. If you're considering leaving, what would help you stay? Who can you confess this to?

10. If you have decided to leave the church, complete this final step. Write down why you are leaving. Now answer this: When you stand before God on the Day of Judgment, will He think that reason is good enough?

7

LOOK TO THE HILLS

I hope you've enjoyed our journey thus far. There's so much we can do to strengthen a faith that has weakened. But in this chapter, we're going to lift our eyes and look to the hills. I'm not referencing the country bumpkin, redneck term. I'm not talking about the mystery of high elevations and those that might dwell there.

When I lived in Arkansas, I learned that when the sun would fall behind the trees, people came down from the hills and invaded the metropolis of Searcy, Arkansas. It was just common knowledge that if you valued your life, you didn't go to Wal-Mart after dark.

When I was a freshman at Harding University, I made the mistake of traveling into these unknown waters. As I was walking down the aisle searching for food like a peasant at 10:00 p. m., I saw something that scarred me forever, something I will never forget—a four-year-old boy with a mullet.

No, I didn't say musket.

I didn't say bullet.

I said mullet.

If you don't know what a mullet is, Google "haircuts in the 1980s that should have never been allowed" (kidding, but seriously). You will see the hideousness of what I'm describing. In the meantime, I will pray for your physical, emotional, and mental well-being.

Now, if you're from Arkansas, please don't take offense to the previous paragraphs. I love your state dearly. In fact, I'm somewhat jealous you get to live there. The Natural State is a wonderful state.

I'm referring to a statement that was probably made by King David, "I lift up my eyes to the hills. From where does my help come? My help comes from the LORD, who made heaven and earth" (Psalm 121:1-2). When mountains won't move, we should lift our eyes to the mountains, the challenges that hover over us day and night. Because even in those demanding, intimidating summits, God dwells.

So how do we *Look to the Hills*?

There's something special about hills and mountains. God used mountains for some of His greatest works of power. God gave Moses the ten commandments, those chiseled words from heaven, on Mt. Sinai. When Elijah battled the prophets of Baal with fire from heaven, the spiritual showdown took place on Mt. Carmel. When Jesus, Moses, and Elijah appeared before Peter, James, and John, it was on a mountain.

If we view Psalm 121 through the lens of a Jewish pilgrim who traveled to Jerusalem once a year for Passover, we can imagine what it would have been like to see those mountains surrounding the city. During the journey, a pilgrim would face the dangers of robbery, challenges of weather, and the weariness of travel. But then, when he walked into the City of David, when he saw the mountains presiding over the city day and night, he knew he was in the presence of God.

Or think about King David. If he did write this psalm, he would have looked at those mountains every day. From his window in the palace, he would have seen God's handiwork providing a natural fortress from oppressors—the same mountains the apostles would have seen a thousand years later, when Jesus said, "If you have faith like a grain of mustard seed, you will say to this mountain, 'Move from here to there,' and it will move" (Matthew 17:20).

Even today, when we climb a mountain and stand on its summit, we feel closer to God. We see the beauty of creation as God sees it. We gain a deeper, heavenly perspective of life.

But even though this psalmist mentions hills, he reminds us that hills, as great as they might be, don't provide what we're looking for. The Psalmist asks, "From where does my help come? My help comes from the LORD, who made heaven and earth" (Psalm 121:1-2). Not the hills, but the One who created them.

Jewish historians wrote about the mountains that hovered over Jerusalem and said that they provided a personal providence, reminding people that God was there. From the highest of heights, help would come.

In Llano, I preached a funeral for a lady who had lived in Llano most of her life. She was buried between Llano and Brady in a small cemetery off Highway 71. Years before, she had purchased a burial plot that looked at the hills (if you want to call them that; these "hills" made ant piles look like Mount Everest). But she chose that plot because she drew comfort from this passage, "My eyes look to the hills," even though they're anthills. She was confused, but she was right. That's the comfort that stems from Psalm 121.

The writer says in v. 5, "The LORD is your keeper; the LORD is your shade on your right hand." And in vv. 7-8, "The LORD will keep you from all evil; he will keep your life. The LORD will keep your going out and your coming in from this time forth and forevermore."

From the summit, God looks down and watches over His people. But even though we can look to the hills and receive help from the Maker of heaven and earth, we often don't. Though the help is at our disposal, we choose not accept it.

I'm convinced that there are three main stages of the Christian faith which help us understand why.

The first stage is, "I want God," like the Rich Young Ruler in Luke 18. We aren't sure who this man was, but he wanted to know what was required for him to "make the cut" for eternal life. He wants the syllabus because he wants God. And it's even apparent that he knows something is missing in his life.

So Jesus answers, "One thing you still lack. Sell all that you have and distribute to the poor" (Luke 18:22). Jesus tells the man to give up the *one* thing that was separating their relationship, but he couldn't do it. He wanted God, but wanting

Him wasn't enough—His desire didn't match the reality of his discipleship.

The next stage is more dedicated than the first. Not "I want God," but "I need God," like the healing of a boy with an evil spirit in Mark 9. Jesus, Peter, James, and John had been on the Mount of Transfiguration. When they rejoined the nine apostles, a large crowd had assembled around them. Jesus asked, "What's going on? Why all the arguing?"

A father spoke up and said, "I brought my son who is suffering from seizures to be healed, and your disciples couldn't do it." I hope this story sounds familiar by now—it's the platform for our book. Jesus shook His head and said, "O unbelieving generation [speaking not only to the crowd but also to His own apostles], how much longer must I put up with you?" (Mark 9:19 NIV)

Jesus had the boy brought to Him. He asked the father, "How long has your son been suffering like this?" The father said, "Since childhood—sometimes this evil spirit throws my son into the water and fire, and tries to kill him." The father looked at Jesus and said, "If you can help, have pity and heal my son! "

Jesus was appalled—He said, "If I can? Everything is possible for he who believes" (Mark 9:23 NIV). That was the father saying, "God, I need you—it's more than a desire, it's a necessity."

What was the problem? The father wasn't sure Jesus could help, which is why he goes on to say, "I do believe, help my unbelief" (Mark 9:24). Jesus looked at the boy and healed him. Jesus did what was needed. But the father still wasn't totally, 100%, surrendered to Jesus.

It's the third stage which is so powerful—not "God, I want you," or "God, I need you", but "God, I can't survive without you"; it's the faith of the Canaanite woman in Matthew 15.

Jesus left Palestine for the first and only time in His ministry and went up to the coast near Tyre and Sidon for a personal time of retreat and refreshment. When He arrived, a woman came to the home where He was staying.

She was a Gentile, an "unbeliever". But for some reason, she believed—she called him "O Lord, Son of David…" (Matthew 15:22), a term proving that she knew He was the Messiah. She pled, "Have mercy on me—my daughter is suffering from demon-possession." Jesus didn't answer her the first time. The disciples even told Jesus to send her away so He could rest. But she kept trying—she kept crying out, "Have mercy on me!" Jesus finally responded. He said, "It is not right to take the children's bread and throw it to the dogs" (Matthew 15:26).

Ouch.

But Jesus wasn't calling her an evil, wicked creature, which is how people viewed dogs in the first century. He used a word that means "puppy." He's saying, "I can't take what belongs to the children and give it to their pets—that wouldn't be right."

But the woman persisted, "Yes, Lord, yet even the dogs eat the crumbs that fall from their masters' table" (Matthew 15:27). In other words, "Don't rob the Jews; let them be filled. But please give me something, because I can't survive without you."

Jesus was more than impressed. During a time of personal refreshment, He stopped to perform a miracle. He even healed her from a distance because the mother proved to Him, "Without you, I am nothing."

Three stages of faith—I Want God, I Need God, I Can't Live Without God. Which stage are *you*?

We can look to the hills all we want, but looking for God and finding God are two completely different things. Until we realize that we're nothing without our King, looking to the hills is wasted energy.

We can all be more like the Canaanite woman. We can all say, "God, give us something, even if it's the crumbs that fall from the table." That's when we realize what faith is all about.

And that's when we can say, "I lift up my eyes to the hills. From where does my help come? My help comes from the LORD, who made heaven and earth" (Psalm 121:1-2).

Look to the hills. The Maker is looking for you.

FOR REFLECTION

1. What "mountains" are currently hovering over your life?

2. Why have these mountains been so challenging?

3. Take a sheet of paper and make three columns, one for each stage. List the attributes that are found in each respective column. What does each stage look like?

4. In which faith-stage are you presently living: I want God, I need God, or I can't survive without God? How do you know?

5. What will it take for you to Look to the Hills this week?

8

CLIMB THE MOUNTAIN

Our entire journey has been guided by Matthew 17:20. If we have faith as small as a mustard seed, we can look at the mountains in the distance, tell them to move, and they will.

I pray that you have enjoyed this book as much as I enjoyed writing it. I truly believe that if you put these steps into practice, you can overcome the trials of life.

In our final chapter together, I'm going to offer one more tip to strengthen that struggling faith. When the mountains won't move, *Climb the Mountain*.

When life hits you in the stomach, stand your ground, and hit back even harder. Conquer those challenges that keep you from reaching your full potential as a child of God.

That sounds really good, doesn't it? But how do we do that?

How do we climb the mountains that challenge our faith?

As we finish our cup of coffee together, let me offer three final tips.

1. CLIMB WITH CONFIDENCE

Confidence is one of the key ingredients for success. If you want to be successful in the work place, it takes confidence. If you want to be successful in your marriage, it takes confidence.

When I went on Wilderness Trek (a seven-night, six-day climb of a mountain, carrying and cooking your own food, sleeping on the ground, and digging your own toilet—not exactly a "relaxing" vacation) the guides told us from day one that it would be impossible to reach the summit without confidence. They said, "If you say to yourself, 'I can't do this,' you won't do it." I thought to myself, "OK, sure, when is that going to happen to me?"

But as the week progressed, and as we walked further and I got hotter and dirtier and crankier, I realized what they meant. When I said, "I can't walk another step," it was like sticking glue to the bottom of my shoes.

If you want to climb the metaphorical mountains of life, it takes even more confidence. That's why Paul reminds us in

Philippians 4:13, "I can do everything through him who gives me strength" (NIV).

Philippians 4:13 is probably one of the most misunderstood verses in the entire Bible. People use it as motivation to accomplish things that don't really matter to God. Seventh-grade boys buy posters of basketball heroes dunking the basketball, and the posters are inscribed with the words, "I can do everything through him who gives me strength."

No you can't. If you're 5'5", 120 lbs, you can't dunk a basketball. I'm six feet tall (my weight doesn't matter), and I can't dunk a basketball. If we can do all things through Christ, then I must not be in Christ. I have as good of a chance at dunking a basketball as Mother Theresa.

Students pray together before they take a test. Have they studied? No. They stayed up late the night before painting toenails or playing video games. But come test time, they say, "I can do all things through Christ who strengthens me." Well, try studying. Christ isn't going take the test for you.

Paul said he could "do all things" after he learned what it meant to be content. Learning that lesson brought many hardships in his life. That's why Paul said, "Christ has helped me do all things through Him."

We can do all things that matter to the righteousness and holiness of God. Christ doesn't care about basketball or test taking. Christ *does* care if we can overcome the world through Him.

The word "do" comes from the Greek word *dunamis*, which means "dynamite." You know about dynamite. It's pretty powerful stuff.

There was a man who was the best fisherman in the county. He would catch fish when no one else would or could. One day, the game warden said, "I want to go fishing with you next week to learn your secret." Well, the expert fisherman graciously agreed and allowed the warden to tag along. They got up early in the morning, got in the boat, and went out to the middle of the lake. The warden said, "So, this is your secret? I always thought coves were better, but you come right out in the middle?" While the warden was talking, the man reached down, opened his tackle box, pulled out a stick of dynamite, lit it, and threw into the lake. "Boom" echoed through the canyon, and the fish rose to the surface. Then he very nonchalantly took his net, scooped them up, and put them in the boat. The game warden said, "Man, are you crazy? You can't do that. This is illegal. Do you not realize who I am? I'm the game warden!

I'm going to have to lock you up!" The whole time the warden was yelling, the man reached back into his tackle box, grabbed another stick of dynamite, lit it, let the fuse burn down real low, handed it to the warden and said, "Are you going to talk, or are you going to fish?"

Dynamite has tremendous power, even when it comes to fishing! But that's the type of power working in us and through us as God's people. It gives us the confidence to climb the challenges of life.

2. CLIMB WITH HUMILITY

It's tough to find a balance between confidence and arrogance, especially when you've accomplished many things. But we often forget that confident people are confident because deep down, they're humble. They realize that pride is one of the most dangerous sins.

The writer of Proverbs said in 16:18, "Pride goes before destruction, a haughty spirit before a fall" (NIV). Every nation in history that was captured during their prime believed they were invincible. Of all the sins, it seems like pride is the one that Satan uses the most to destroy good people.

When Jesus challenged the Pharisees in Matthew 23 with

the seven woes, pride was the main point of His sermon. He said in v. 12, "Whoever exalts himself will be humbled, and whoever humbles himself will be exalted." Jesus was speaking to teachers who were attaching extra assignments, traditions of men, onto God's syllabus for righteousness. They were proud and arrogant; they puffed out their chest because they thought they had everything figured out, and they believed that it was their job to correct the spiritual ignorance of hopeless humanity. But Jesus said, "Be very careful—you aren't as spiritual as you think you are. You might know the facts. You might have memorized the rules. But when I see you, I don't see progress. I see *pride*."

When we climb the mountains of life—the challenges of faith—we can't be arrogant. We have confidence because of Jesus, but we can't think that we have every answer. We're nothing without Him. Only those who climb with this understanding move mountains. And we find the balance between confidence and humility by...

3. CLIMBING WITH EXPECTATION
OF GOD-GIVEN SUCCESS

It's not the success that we create, but the success that we receive. It's the success found in Philippians 3:12-14. Just look at the order of everything Paul mentions in this passage.

He begins by saying, "Not that I have already obtained this" (Philippians 3:12). We ask, "Obtained what, Paul?" The previous verses give the answer: knowing the power of Jesus' resurrection, the fellowship of sharing in His sufferings, becoming like Him in His death, and attaining the resurrection of the dead (vv. 10-11).

Even Paul, a man who went on three missionary journeys, wrote 13 letters of the New Testament, and challenged Jews and Gentiles to open debates, didn't believe that he was as spiritually mature as he needed to be. That's humility at its best.

But then Paul says, "I press on"—and this is how—"I forget about what is behind me" (Philippians 3:13). Paul often used track and field as an example for Christian faith. A runner can't look back and keep his stride. We can't live in the past and succeed in the present. Dwelling on failure is detrimental, but dwelling on success is just as destructive. We must advance.

So Paul said that he "pressed on" (NIV), focusing his mind on new possibilities and devoting his energy to the glory of God. And when he moved forward, he had the goal of winning the prize (Philippians 3:14). There's the expectation of success. Paul doesn't say, "I have the goal of the prize." He says, "I have the goal of winning the prize. I know that something will be given to me."

But he reminds us what that "something" is—the prize that calls him "heavenward in Christ Jesus" (Philippians 3:14 NIV). It's not an earthly trophy, worldly accolade, or executive title. It's the privilege and blessing of going home to be with God. That's what climbing mountains is all about, and that's how we climb them.

We confess that we aren't as spiritually mature as we need to be.

We forget what's behind.

We press on for what's ahead.

And in the end, we know that we win a life with God.

The mountains and challenges of life are very real. They come at different times and in different ways. But regardless of their form or function, they stand tall, hovering over our emotions and intimidating every move. But if you haven't heard anything I've said in this entire book, please hear this:

The mountains don't have to win!

The only power that the mountains have is the power that we give them. Through the mercy of God, we can conquer any crisis. God walks with us hand in hand. And one day, we will look back and see how far we've come.

You might be familiar with the name Glenn Cunningham. Cunningham was a great distance runner, an American Olympian, known as the "Kansas Flyer." In 1934, he set a world record for running the mile in four minutes and six seconds. But do you know why that record is so incredible? For the majority of Cunningham's life, he was paralyzed.

In 1919, when he was eight years old, there was a large explosion at his school. He lost flesh on his knees and toes on his feet. Doctors said he would never walk again. They wanted to amputate his legs, but Cunningham was so distressed, his parents wouldn't allow it. Cunningham was determined.

He learned to walk again in his back yard by stretching out his arms and pulling on one fence post at a time, until he could gain enough strength to stand. This process continued for months until finally this man, who was told that he would never walk again, ran a mile faster than any man before him.

Cunningham proved that the impossible was possible.

When we talk about moving mountains on our own, the conversation is based on an impossible possibility. We don't have the talent or ability to pull it off. That's why the world crashes and burns when they try. But because of Jesus, and because of our all-powerful, all-loving Father in Heaven, we, like Cunningham, prove that the impossible is possible. Lean on God each and every day, regardless of the challenge. That's when the mountains move, and that's when your faith survives. I believe in you. God believes in you.

Move those mountains!

FOR REFLECTION

1. If you tried to move mountains in the past but failed, why did it happen?

2. In what ways can you be more confident?

3. In what ways can you be more humble?

4. Expecting God-given success—what does this look like?

5. What impacted you the most in this book? Why?

6. Who can you share this book with?

7. How can I, the author, pray for you or help you? Feel free to send prayer requests to jacob@rscoc.org.

ABOUT THE AUTHOR

J acob Hawk serves as the Pulpit Minister for Riverside Church of Christ in Kerrville, Texas. He holds both bachelor and master's degrees in Bible from Harding University in Searcy, Arkansas. He speaks at seminars and lectureships around the United States and television programs in the Texas Hill Country. In addition to his writing, Jacob has a burning passion to preach the gospel that he first discovered at the age of nine years old when he delivered his first sermon. Jacob and his wife, Natalie, have two sons, Hayden and Hudson.

Made in the USA
Charleston, SC
20 December 2014